TRIALS AND SENTENCES

Zachary A. Kelly

The Rourke Corporation, Inc.
Vero Beach, Florida 32964

PHOTO CREDITS:
© Ed Carlin/Archive Photo: cover; © Matthew McVay/Stock Boston: page 4; © Bob Daemmrich/Stock Boston: pages 6, 21; East Coast Studios: pages 9, 12, 22, 27, 40, 44; Tony Gray: pages 14, 28; © Stacy Pick/Stock Boston: pages 16, 30;
© David Woo/Stock Boston: page 18; Danny Bachelor: pages 24, 43

PRODUCED BY: East Coast Studios, Merritt Island, Florida

EDITORIAL SERVICES:
Penworthy Learning Systems
          .

Library of Congress Cataloging-in-Publication Data

Kelly, Zachary A., 1970-
    Trials and sentences / by Zachary Kelly.
        p. cm. — (Law and order)
    Includes index.
    Summary: Explains elements of the judicial process including civil and criminal court trials, the roles of judges and juries, degrees of criminality, and ways in which restitution can be enforced.
        ISBN 0-86593-576-9
    1. Trials—United States Juvenile literature. 2. Procedure (Law)—United States Juvenile literature. [1. Trials. 2. Law.] I. Title. II. Series.
KF8910.K45   1999
347.73'7—dc21   99-28690
                                                                       CIP

Printed in the USA

TABLE OF CONTENTS

A judge oversees all court trials.

CHAPTER ONE

WHAT HAPPENS IN A COURT TRIAL?

Most lawsuits end before they go to trial. Sometimes, though, a case must go to the court to be settled. A **trial** is a meeting in court to find who is at fault in a case and decide what that person has to do about it. In a **criminal trial**, the case centers on a crime for which the **defendant** has been accused. The court hears evidence about the crime, decides on the defendant's guilt or innocence; and, if guilty, gives the defendant a sentence, telling him or her what to do. A **civil trial** centers on a disagreement between two people or groups of people. The court hears both sides and then decides who is at fault and what that person has to do.

An attorney questions potential jurors.

The steps are similar in civil and criminal court trials. After talking before the trial, the attorneys for each side help to select a jury. Then both sides give opening statements about their cases to the court. They question witnesses and give evidence. Attorneys also stand out against evidence that does not seem to fit the case. When they are finished giving evidence, the attorneys give their closing statements and rest their cases. Next, the judge or jury thinks about the evidence. A jury talks over the case among themselves. They then give the decision to the court. The jury might take 15 minutes or several months, depending on how complicated the case is.

An important idea in a court trial is called the **burden of proof**. Whoever has the burden of proof must prove that their side of the case is correct. In U.S. criminal courts, the **prosecution** always has the burden of proof, because a suspect is innocent until proven guilty. The prosecution's job is to prove that the defendant is guilty. All that a defendant has to do is show reasonable doubt that he or she committed the crime. In civil trials, both sides have the burden of proof.

Law & Order Facts

"A society that values the good name and freedom of every individual should not condemn a person for commission of a crime when there is a reasonable doubt about his or her guilt..." Inre Winship, 1970

Attorneys sometimes study historic cases when preparing for a trial.

A verdict of guilty or not guilty comes at the end of a criminal trial. Often a jury decides whether the accused is guilty, but in trials without juries, judges decide. Usually the judge then gives a sentence, which is the punishment a criminal receives when found guilty. In a civil trial the jury states whether the **plaintiff** or the defendant is in the wrong. Judgments in civil trials often include **restitution** for the winner of the case. Restitution is often money or a service of some kind, that the loser must give to the winner to make up for the damage done.

CHAPTER TWO

BEFORE THE JUDGE

The sixth amendment allows all defendants to have a jury trial if they want one. Not all defendants use that right. If a defendant chooses not to have a jury trial, the case is brought in front of the judge alone. A case by a judge, not a jury, is called a bench trial. In civil cases, defendants also have the right to a bench trial. Bench trials are common in civil cases. Some civil cases have been settled before trial, but they need a judge to make them legal. Many divorces use bench trials.

Some before-trial hearings require a judge. A defendant comes before a judge at an **arraignment**.

A judge decides on a defendant's bail.

The arraignment is a defendant's first hearing after being arrested. At the arraignment, a defendant hears the charge against him or her. The defendant also makes a plea about his or her guilt. After hearing a plea, the judge sets an amount of money for bail and tells the defendant of the right to an attorney, the right to remain silent, and the right to reasonable bail. The judge's job in an arraignment is to tell the defendant what he or she is accused of, to explain the defendant's rights, and to set bail at an amount reasonable for the crime.

Bail is money given to the court so that a defendant does not have to stay in jail while waiting for trial. If the defendant shows up for the trial, the bail money is given back. If the defendant does not show up, the court keeps the money. Sometimes a judge may not set bail because he or she believes that the defendant will not return for trial. This usually happens only in cases concerning very serious crimes or repeat offenders. If the judge does not set bail, then the defendant must wait in jail until the trial.

After an arraignment, a defendant may see the judge again before trial, at a **preliminary hearing**. A preliminary hearing is also with a judge only.

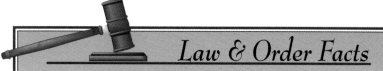

Law & Order Facts

The title of a judge is "The Honorable...."
For example, a judge named Alice Robinson would be called "The Honorable Alice Robinson."

A police officer prepares physical evidence that will be used by the prosecution.

The judge reviews the charge against the defendant and the amount of bail. Then the prosecution states its case against the defendant and explains how it is going to try to prove him or her guilty. The judge's job is to look over the evidence that the prosecution wants to use and make sure it is acceptable for the trial. If it is not, the judge may not allow the prosecution to use it. The judge also makes sure there is enough evidence to show that the defendant might be guilty. If there is not enough evidence, the judge may dismiss (stop) the case.

A court swears in a jury that will decide a criminal case.

CHAPTER THREE

BEFORE THE JURY

In most states, a defendant has to ask for a trial by jury. If the defendant does not ask, then he or she will have a bench trial in front of a judge. Defendants often want a jury trial because it usually seems fairer. A jury is an average group of citizens helping to judge another average citizen, accused of a crime. A jury's job is to study the facts of a case and discuss them until they all agree on a verdict.

The court selects the jury before the trial. First they make a list of about 1,000 people in the area, chosen at random (by chance).

Will these jurors be acceptable for the attorney's case? The lawyer's questions will find out.

From that list, they choose a few hundred names, also at random. Then they narrow the list even more, and send jury duty notices. A jury duty notice tells a citizen to go to court to sit on a jury. People must be qualified to sit on a jury. A juror must be a U.S. citizen, at least 18 years old. He or she must be able to see, hear, and speak well, and to speak and understand English. The attorneys for both sides usually talk with each juror. They want to make sure no one has ideas that would keep him or her from making a fair judgment.

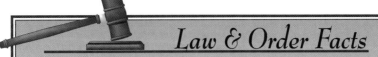

During a jury trial, attorneys are not worried about convincing the judge that their side is the right side. They are speaking to the jury. Attorneys often think of the jury as they prepare evidence to give. They may use pictures and emotional testimony (a witness who cries while answering questions for example) to win the jury over. In most courtrooms, the jury sits in a large booth on the side, watching everything. They will often take notes about the trial to use later. If a juror has a question, he or she can write it down and ask the judge about it after the day's hearing.

The jury's job is to make a decision after studying the facts of the trial. After the trial, jurors move to a backroom to discuss the case with each other. They choose a spokesperson, called the foreperson. The foreperson talks to the judge about questions, takes votes, and reads the verdict in court once the jury reaches a decision.

Jurors may take notes throughout a trial. These notes may help them decide if the defendant is guilty.

In most states, 12 people make up a jury; and everyone has to agree to the verdict. After everyone votes the same, the foreperson reads the verdict in court; and the judge gives the defendant a sentence.

A judge prepares to sentence an accused person.

CHAPTER FOUR

CRIMINAL TRIAL

The sixth amendment states that "in all criminal prosecutions, the accused shall enjoy the right to a speedy and public trial by an impartial jury." The courts work hard to carry out that amendment. Most states require the court to try a suspect no more than 150 days after his or her arrest. The public and newspeople may attend almost every trial, though a judge may sometimes limit news coverage. A defendant must ask for a jury trial. If the accused asks, then the court selects people in the area to serve on the jury.

A defense attorney pleads the case for his client at a bench trial.

Over half of the states require 12-member juries who must come to complete agreement about a verdict. (Defendants also have the right to request a bench trial, which is a trial without a jury).

A criminal trial follows a number of steps. The jury is called and sworn in, which means the jury members vow to be truthful and honest as they judge the defendant. Then the court reads the charge against the defendant. The prosecution begins the trial with an opening statement. An opening statement describes the case against the defendant. The defense may then present its

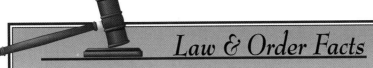

opening statement, or it can wait until the prosecution presents its entire case. Now, the prosecution begins giving evidence, by questioning witnesses and showing physical evidence, like fingerprints or weapons found at the scene. When the prosecution is finished questioning a witness, the defense may then cross-examine the witness. That is, the defense may ask questions in support of the defendant.

The prosecution must present a well-organized case against the defendant. The defense does not have to. The defense may skip presenting their side if they think the prosecution's case did not convince the jury. If the defense does present their case, it follows the pattern set by the prosecution: opening statement, questioning of witnesses, and presentation of physical evidence.

An attorney makes her closing argument to a jury.

The prosecution has the right to a rebuttal, or response, after the defense presents its case. In the rebuttal, the prosecution tries to weaken the defense's case by pointing out its flaws. The defense may then respond once to the prosecution's rebuttal, trying to weaken the prosecution's case. Both sides then make closing statements, which are summaries of the case. The jury then leaves the court to decide the verdict.

A bailiff stands watch over a courtroom.

A police officer catches a driver speeding. Speeding is a traffic infraction.

CHAPTER FIVE

THREE KINDS OF CRIME

Crime causes damage by hurting property and people. Some crimes are more serious than others and deserve much stronger punishments. Take the rules in a home, for instance. It may be against the rules for a child to slam a door, run down the hallway, or light a match without an adult present. Each situation could cause a different amount of harm, and most parents would have a different punishment for each situation.

A person who commits a felony usually spends time in prison.

The same is true for crimes in U.S. law. The courts divide crimes into three kinds. A crime is either an **infraction**, a **misdemeanor**, or a **felony**. An infraction (like a parking ticket) is punished with a small fine or, sometimes, a small amount of community service. Infractions almost never make it to a court trial. Misdemeanors cause more damage than infractions and usually get much stronger punishments. Felonies harm people and property the most. Punishments for felonies are often very harsh. Misdemeanors and felonies often draw fines, community service, or even prison.

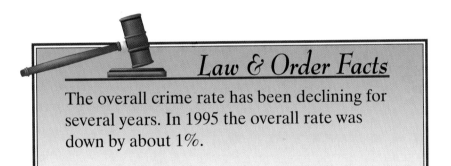

Law & Order Facts

The overall crime rate has been declining for several years. In 1995 the overall rate was down by about 1%.

The people who made our laws held that certain crimes, like murder and robbery, are always wrong. They called these crimes *mala in se*, which is Latin for "bad in itself." Today we call them *mala in se* crimes. Other crimes that do not seem to cause so much harm are called *mala prohibita*, or "wrong because prohibited." *Mala prohibita* is the Latin name for what we call misdemeanors.

Misdemeanors include petty theft (taking things of small value), trespassing (going onto another's land wrongfully), and gambling (betting on games of chance where such is illegal). A police officer cannot arrest someone for a misdemeanor unless the officer has a **warrant** or saw the suspect commit the crime. Suspects usually settle misdemeanor charges outside of court. The sentence for the charge depends on the person's record and the crime. The stiffest sentence for a misdemeanor is a year in a local jail and a fine.

Arson, setting fire to a building, is a felony.

Felonies include murder (unlawful killing of a human being), arson (setting fire to another's property), and armed robbery (taking another's property by force while carrying a weapon). If an officer suspects that someone is committing a felony nearby, the officer may arrest the suspect. Police do not need a warrant to arrest for a felony if they have reasonable suspicion or the victim made a statement. Defendants in felony cases often take care of their case out of court by pleading guilty or making a plea bargain. Sentences for felony crimes range anywhere from one year in prison to death.

CHAPTER SIX

CIVIL TRIAL

When someone commits a crime, the state prosecutes the suspect by taking him or her to court. This kind of trial, a criminal trial, is between a person and the state; and it focuses on a specific crime. When two people or businesses have a serious disagreement, they can take their problem to court, even if it does not involve a crime. The kind of trial that focuses on a conflict between two people is called a civil trial.

A plaintiff's attorney prepares papers to be sent to the defendant.

The main purpose of a civil trial is to review the facts and the laws that relate to the case and see if someone is at fault. If one person owes another by law, the court will rule in favor of the person who is to receive the money. The court will give the debtor (person who owes) a plan for paying.

The person who claims that he or she is owed something is called the plaintiff. The person the plaintiff takes to court is the defendant. The plaintiff begins a case by entering a **complaint.** A complaint tells how much the defendant owes (according to the

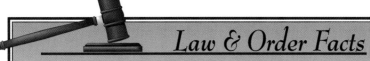

plaintiff) and how the plaintiff wants to be repaid. After entering a complaint with the court, the plaintiff sends a summons to the defendant, telling the defendant what the case is about and when to arrive in court. Sometimes the defendant will settle the case at this point without going to court. The plaintiff wins the case. The defendant then must pay restitution to the plaintiff. Restitution is the amount the court says the plaintiff deserves.

Most of the time, a plaintiff and defendant work to settle the case out of court. They send letters and other papers back and forth and discuss certain facts about the case. The plaintiff and defendant also work with the laws that deal with their disagreement. If people do not settle through these steps, the case moves to trial. The steps of a civil trial are close to a criminal trial, except that both people try to prove something in a civil trial. A civil trial includes a jury, if requested by the defendant.

A civil case moves like a criminal case through opening statements, evidence, cross-examination, and closing arguments. At two points during the trial, the judge can stop (dismiss) the case for lack of evidence: after the plaintiff presents evidence and before the closing arguments. If the trial lasts to the end, then the jury or judge gives a verdict, which explains how the defendant is to make restitution.

CHAPTER SEVEN

SENTENCE AND REPAYMENT

When a court finds a defendant guilty at the end of a trial, it gives a verdict and a sentence. The verdict states the defendant's guilt and the charge. The sentence tells the defendant what he or she must do to make up for the crime (criminal case) or fault (civil case). The purpose of the sentence is to give the defendant a way to make restitution, to pay back society or an individual for the crime or fault committed.

Community service hours can be served in many ways, including picking up litter.

A judge, with many options for sentencing, keeps several things in mind. For example, the harshness of a a sentence must match the nature of the crime. Also, a sentence should allow the criminal to pay back some of the damage done. A judge often forms an opinion of a defendant's attitude and character and sorrow for the crime. If so, the judge may use that opinion to come up with a fair sentence. A judge may also assign community service hours, during which a criminal works for the state, or a judge may put a criminal in jail for a time. Sometimes, the defendant's sentence may be a fine—an amount of money to be paid to the state or an injured party.

In civil cases, a judge considers the fault of both the plaintiff and the defendant. A judge may go with the restitution the plaintiff claims (asks for) if it matches the defendant's rights in the case. If the defendant makes a counterclaim (a claim for restitution against the plaintiff), then the judge may go with it instead of or along with the plaintiff's claim.

A judge listens to both sides of a civil case before making a decision.

Passing through a metal detector to enter a courthouse

GLOSSARY

arraignment (uh RAYN munt) — meeting of accused person and a criminal court judge in which the accused answers the charge against him or her

burden of proof (BER dn uv PROOF) — job of proving a charge

civil trial (SIV ul TRIE ul) — a court trial held in civil court according to civil law

complaint (kuhm PLAYNT) — paper setting forth a plaintiff's request for restitution in a civil case

criminal trial (KRIM uh nul TRIE ul) — a court trial held in criminal court according to criminal law

defendant (di FEN dunt) — accused in a criminal or civil case

felony (FEL uh nee) — most serious kind of crime carrying a harsh punishment; examples: murder, armed robbery

infraction (in FRAC shun) — least serious kind of crime; example: parking or speeding ticket

mala in se (MAL uh in SAY) — "bad in itself" crimes such as murder that are bad at all times and in all places; felonies

GLOSSARY

mala prohibita (MAL uh pro HIB it uh) — "bad because prohibited," crimes less serious than felony that are bad because they are against the law; misdemeanors

misdemeanor (MISS di MEE nur) — crime more serious than an infraction but less serious than a felony; examples: petty theft, trespassing

plaintiff (PLAYN tif) — person or group that starts a court case by sending a complaint (civil court) or arresting (criminal court)

preliminary hearing (preh LIM uh NER ee HEER ing) — pretrial meeting in court for going over the charge, bail, and the prosecutor's case

prosecution (PRAHS i KYOO shun) — the person or people responsible for prosecuting a defendant in court

restitution (RES ti TOO shun) — money for loss, damage, or injury

trial (TRIE ul) — a legal proceeding held in a court of law to determine the guilt or innocence of a defendant and to sentence the defendant if he or she is found guilty

warrant (WAWR unt) — paper giving an officer the right to search, seize, arrest, or make judgment

FURTHER READING

- Brown, Lawrence. *The Supreme Court.* Washington, D.C.: Congressional Quarterly, 1981.
- Conklin, John E. *Criminology.* Allyn and Bacon: Needham Heights, Mass, 1995.
- De Sola, Ralph. *Crime Dictionary.* NY: Facts on File, 1988.
- Hill, Gerald and Hill, Kathleen. *Real Life Dictionary of the Law.* Los Angeles: General Publishing Group, 1995.
- Janosik, Robert ., ed. *Encyclopedia of the American Judicial System.* NY: Charles Scribner and Sons, 1987.
- Johnson, Loch K. *America's Secret Power (CIA).* Oxford: OUP, 1989.
- Kadish, Sanford H., ed. *Encyclopedia of Crime and Justice.* NY: The Free Press, 1983.
- McShane, M. and Williams, F., eds. *Encyclopedia of American Prisons.* NY: Garland, 1996.
- Morris, N. and Rothman, D., eds. *The Oxford History of the Prison.* Oxford: OUP, 1995.
- Regoli, Robert and Hewitt, John. *Criminal Justice.* Prentice-Hall: Englewood Cliffs, NJ, 1996.
- Renstrum, Peter G. *The American Law Dictionary.* Santa Barbara, CA: ABC-CLIO, 1991.
- Territo, Leonard, et al. *Crime & Justice in America.* West: St. Paul, MN, 1995.
- *The Constitution of the United States.* Available in many editions.
- *The Declaration of Independence.* Available in many editions.
- Voigt, Linda, et al. *Criminology and Justice.* McGraw-Hill: New York, 1994.

- http://entp.hud.gov/comcrime.html
  Crime Prevention
  Department of Justice
  PAVNET (Partnership Against Violence Network)
  Justice Information Center
- http://www.fightcrime.com/lcrime.htm
  Safety and Security Connection
  The Ultimate Guide to Safety and Security
  Resources on the Internet
- http://www.internets.com/spolice.htm
  Police Databases
- http://www.psrc.com/lkfederal.html
  Links to most Federal Agencies
- http://www.dare-america.com/
  Official Website of D.A.R.E.

INDEX